Tackle tennis
TONY MOTTRAM

Tackle tennis

TONY MOTTRAM

STANLEY PAUL/LONDON

Stanley Paul & Co Ltd
3 Fitzroy Square, London W1

An Imprint of the Hutchinson Publishing Group

London Melbourne Sydney Auckland
Wellington Johannesburg Cape Town
and agencies throughout the world

First published 1971 as Play Better Tennis
This Edition 1975
© Yorkshire Television 1971, 1975
Photographs by A. B. Cole, Tennis World Magazine

Set in Monotype Times
Printed in Great Britain by Flarepath Printers Ltd,
St Albans, Herts, and bound by Wm Brendon & Son Ltd,
of Tiptree, Essex

ISBN 0 09 124760 8 (Cased)
ISBN 0 09 124761 6 (Paper)

CONTENTS

ACTION STRIPS

By flicking through the pages of this book the World's leading players can be seen in action making the basic tennis strokes.

Flick forwards from page 19 to see the action strips on the right-hand pages.

Flick backwards from page 102 to see the action strips on left-hand pages.

INTRODUCTION

Lawn tennis is in a most important and interesting stage of its development. Since it became open to professionals in 1968 the publicity which the major events and leading players have attracted has encouraged the development of the game throughout the world. The teaching of players of all ages in schools and in clubs has not however kept pace with this explosion of interest. There are too few qualified coaches and they cannot cope with the numbers involved.

Although many players develop their games without any coaching at all, it is now recognized that few players are able to reach the limit of their capabilities without guidance. As higher levels of play are reached the game becomes more and more a specialized technique.

The game is more rewarding when you can play it well, and certainly more exciting as improvement can be felt. To a great extent, though, progress becomes more difficult when players' strokes have not been built upon a sound foundation. Habits once acquired against a moving ball are hard to change.

The game is entering an era of rapidly rising standards. From the international stage right down through tournaments and regional levels to play in clubs and at schools, higher standards are being demanded and achieved.

This book has been written in the hope that it may help to bridge the gap in coaching which exists for a multitude of enthusiasts. The male gender has been used throughout only for convenience, and the instructions are equally applicable to women's tennis. Similarly, the left-hander will need to reverse the instructions where appropriate since the text has been prepared only for right-handed players.

1 Choosing your equipment

So many players use equipment that is unsuited for them that a few words on some of the points to remember when buying it may not be out of place at the start.

As a general rule avoid buying cheap unbranded goods. They often appear to be good value but nearly always prove to be more expensive in the long run. Rackets, shoes, balls and clothing that are made by reputable firms always give good service. Your racket for instance must be selected with care. The cost will vary mainly in the frame construction and according to the stringing. It is a mistake to think that if you buy the most expensive racket it is bound to last you longer than a cheaper one. When you pay over £10 for a racket you are buying performance as much as durability. The natural gut strings in rackets of this price account for nearly half their cost. Yet gut which is still the most resilient string in this modern age is far less durable than certain synthetic strings of lower performance.

If you are a beginner then use a synthetically strung racket to start with. This is quite adequate for your purpose and the synthetic strings have the added advantage over gut insofar that the strings are impervious to moisture which means you can play on wet days or when the balls are damp. Gut quickly softens and fractures under these conditions. The advantage of gut for the better player is in its greater response and wider 'sweet spot' when strung to a high tension.

The weight, balance and grip size are the next most important points to keep in mind when choosing a racket. Too light a racket may feel easy to swing in the sports shop but may be incapable of doing its job properly for you in controlling the ball. It will also have a less sturdy frame than one that is heavier. On the other hand a heavy racket may be too tiring to swing and may make you late on your shots under pressure. As a rough guide young players of average height and build from 14 to 16 or 17 years of age will find rackets of $13\frac{1}{4}$ to $13\frac{1}{2}$ ozs., evenly balanced, to be most suitable. These weights correspond to racket notations of "light" or "light medium". Men and women of average height and build will find that rackets marked "light medium" or "medium" are most suitable for them. Only players of above average strength and build or experience should consider using heavier rackets.

For children up to about 13, there are special junior rackets. These are lighter in weight than senior models and slightly shorter. In all other respects, though, they

10

are normal rackets and they greatly help the developing young player to produce sounder strokes in readiness for the later transition to the lightest senior racket.

Grip sizes and shapes depend on players' hands and also the way in which they locate their fingers on the handle for the various grips. Again as a rough guide, a grip of $4\frac{1}{2}''$ is suitable for the smaller hand, while a $5''$ grip would be better for the man with a large hand. So far as shape is concerned rackets are now made with standard grips of varying circumference which suit the vast majority of players. A slightly flattened shape sometimes appeals to the player who likes to place the thumb firmly across the grip for the backhand because it then provides a wider platform for the thumb to develop its bracing effect.

Wood or metal?

In the past few years metal rackets have made their impact on the game and are likely to gain in general popularity as more and more of the top players use them. They have one big advantage which is in their thin streamlined frame-form which allows the racket to be moved through the air more easily. This advantage is most clearly felt by the player when serving, but many leading players also feel that they are more difficult to use for the drives. My own

11

experience with them makes me feel that metal rackets have an overall advantage but only in the hands of highly experienced players who are competent to control them. For this reason I cannot see that they benefit the beginner or ordinary club player very much.

It is important however to try and play with the best balls you can afford. They are expensive but controlled tennis becomes more and more difficult as balls lose their nap. Once they are smooth your tennis is severely handicapped.

Shoes are another important item. They should fit comfortably and securely. Avoid using the light flimsy type. Your feet will tire more quickly in them than when you wear more substantial ones with heavier soles and an inbuilt cushion support. The sole pattern is also another point to consider. A completely smooth sole will not provide a satisfactory foothold on loose-surface hard courts and may also slip on grass if it is the slightest bit damp. The general preference these days for outdoor tennis is for a serrated sole pattern. A smoother sole is better on wood indoors.

Clothing should be comfortable and not distracting. There are now special socks with a woollen insole made for tennis players that protect the feet and help to avoid blisters. Shirts, shorts, skirts or dresses should all allow full freedom of movement. Nothing is worse than a garment which pulls at your body or swirls out in a breeze to tangle with your racket on an important point. Wear clothes that are smart and make you feel good but allow you to forget them so that you can give the game your full concentration.

2 The fundamentals

Whether you are a Wimbledon champion or the rawest beginner your form depends on the degree to which you obey the fundamentals of the game. Champions know this and never cease to practice to perfect them. Many players however are unaware of the basic requirements and a little time spent in appreciating their importance and value can encourage and develop "thinking" players whose improvement and progress will usually outstrip those who cannot be bothered to get to grips mentally with their game.

To play better tennis you must learn:
1 To keep your eye on the ball.
2 Sound footwork.
3 Good balance.
4 To control the racket swing.
5 To control the racket face.
6 To concentrate.

Learn to keep your eye on the ball

This is the most important fundamental of all, for without watching the ball it is impossible to play. There are good and poor watchers of the ball and your own personal ability in this respect is shown each time you attempt a shot. If the ball normally comes off the strings sweetly then you are obeying this fundamental – even though the ball may not go where you intend. If many of your shots, however, feel harsh on the racket, or if you sometimes find yourself playing the ball "off the wood" – or even worse missing it completely – then you have not mastered the technique.

Consider the problem that is involved. For most of the rally the ball is in front of the player and travelling relatively slowly towards him. As the player positions himself to take it at the side of the body, its relative speed increases until the moment the ball is struck. It is very much like watching an approaching express roar through a station.

The eye is like the lens of a camera. If it is not fast enough it will be unable to retain a clear image of the ball in the all-important last three feet of its flight to the impact position. A great deal of conscious effort in watching the ball is needed by the tennis player before the eye can learn to retain a sharp outline of the ball just before the hit. A useful tip to remember is to look for the seam that runs around the ball and to keep looking until the ball vanishes from view.

Sound footwork

This is the fundamental to which most common errors can be traced. Not only

15

ROGER
TAYLOR
SERVICE
STROKE

EVONNE
GOOLAGONG
BACKHAND
DRIVE

EVONNE
GOOLAGONG
SERVICE
STROKE

CHARLIE
PASARELL
BACKHAND
DRIVE

must the player move quickly to arrive in good time in the hitting area, but once there must, whenever possible, produce the footwork pattern that allows the stroke to be produced with greatest effect.

The ability to move quickly is of the utmost importance, but much of its value is lost if the footwork is slovenly or badly formed. It is for this reason that I always encourage my pupils to develop the basic footwork patterns for the forehand and backhand drives first from standing positions alongside the racket stroke production. When these patterns have been well established as habits without conscious thought, they begin to reproduce themselves at the end of each moving approach to the ball and the basis of sound footwork has been established. The method is described on pages 47 and 60.

Good balance

This means the control of the player's bodyweight to enable it to be used in the most effective way. Good balance assists the player's control and power by allowing the racket face to remain in contact with the ball for a longer time while the bodyweight moves forwards parallel to the line of flight of the ball. Good balance depends on the player's position and to a great extent it is the forerunner of a successful stroke.

16

Control of the racket swing

Top class players do not have to think about the way to swing the racket for their various strokes. For them the actions have become habitual and therefore consistent. A considerable amount of thought however must be given to the production of the various strokes by the beginner and developing player. Slowly but surely with practice they will become automatic and repeat themselves without conscious thought. Unfortunately unsound methods can just as easily develop habitually as sound ones. It is for this reason that beginners in particular should ensure that their methods are sound during the formative years.

Players should try to retain clear mental pictures of the different racket actions for the basic strokes. They are:

1 For the service and overhead smash the *head* of the racket should the "*thrown*" *through* the ball.

2 In the forehand and backhand drives the racket should be "*swung*" *through* the ball.

3 In low volleying where control is more important than speed, the racket should be "*pushed*" *through* the ball.

4 In volleying the higher ball where speed can be used more safely, the racket should be "*punched*" *through* the ball.

This side view of Roger Taylor's service shows the way that top players 'lean in' as the service is made to give them a flying start on their way to the net for their volleying attacks.

The exciting young Australian Evonne Goolagong has a firm but free-flowing backhand drive. The points to note are her footwork and the full turn of her shoulders as the stroke is prepared. The finish emphasises the fine balance.

Evonne Goolagong possesses a beautifully rhythmical service swing. The path of the racket from impact shows that this was an almost flat-hit service. Her balance throughout is perfect – proof of a correctly positioned throw-up of the ball.

Charlie Pasarell of America has a smoothly produced and effective backhand drive. He locks his wrist through the ball, and perfect balance in the finish allows him to recover quickly to the original 'ready' position.

17

Control of the racket face

The face of the racket must be brought to the ball at the required angle if the shot is to be correctly played both in height and direction.

Anyone who has had the unpleasant experience of being hit with a fast travelling tennis ball during play will recall the heaviness of the ball at impact. The racket strings are continually subject to this impact weight which tends to press the head of the racket backwards. Similarly the ball has only to be met the slightest bit above or below the sweet spot and it begins to exert a twisting effect on the racket. Few players exert the degree of wrist control that is necessary to maintain the correct angle of the racket face. A loose wrist is often the cause of loss of control.

For the beginner, the best way of visualizing the angle of the racket face is to think how you would first use the palm of your hand in playing the ball with the forehand drive and service actions. When this is appreciated the racket face can be visualized as a large hand for these strokes. For the backhand drive consider how you would use the back of your hand for the stroke. Then introduce the racket face for the backhand action in the same way.

This of course is simple stuff. Things become more involved with the use of spin

18

when the strings must strike the ball a glancing blow. Although it is necessary to keep your eyes on the ball as it approaches, the player must develop an *awareness* of the position of the racket face as the stroke is made.

Concentration

This is the fundamental which governs a player's form and rate of progress. No outside thoughts must be allowed to intrude during play and practice if worthy results are to be achieved. Concentration can be mastered and deepened with continual effort and it is a most vital part of the correct state of mind for winning.

3 Gripping the racket

The way you hold your racket plays an important part in the formation of the various strokes. While it may be possible for a talented player to overcome the handicap of unsound grips, these restrict performance and limit the player's capabilities.

The forehand drive grip

The vast majority of first class players use what is called the eastern or "*shake-hands*" grip for the forehand drive. This allows the face of the racket to be presented vertically to the ball (refer back to control of the racket face in Chapter 1) yet to retain a good degree of adaptability.

The name of this grip describes it perfectly because the hand is placed around the handle as though shaking hands with it. The illustration on page 21 shows the positioning of the fingers and thumb.

One of the most common errors with beginners is to bunch the fingers. The forefinger should be extended slightly as though gripping the trigger of a gun, and there should be a slight separation of the second and third fingers. Spreading the fingers in this way discourages wristiness. The aim is to swing the racket as an exten-

20

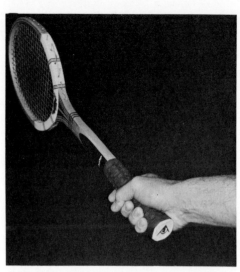

The Eastern forehand 'shake-hands' grip
The hand is behind the handle where it can exert considerable firmness and power to the stroke.

sion of the arm and players who have been used to bunching the fingers will find a certain stiffness in the stroke which will feel strange initially. The advantage of spreading the forefinger is in the greater control it gives over the racket face and the way it encourages a proper swing from the shoulder. When players have mastered this grip they will be well advised to check its accuracy from time to time. If you are using a suitable grip size for your hand, the

21

tips of the last three fingers should locate themselves on the flat of the leading face of the leather grip. Use a few minutes of an occasional practice session to "feel" for the correct location of the fingers as you switch grips for the backhand and forehand drives.

The backhand drive grips

In the majority of cases where players find difficulty in playing or developing their backhand drives, the problem can be traced back to unsound grips. A change of grip is necessary from the forehand "shakehands" grip if an uninhibited stroke is to be developed. From the forehand grip which places the palm of the hand behind the handle, the change is anti-clockwise so that the palm is located on top of the handle with the strings vertical to the ground. This positioning of the hand places the thumb behind the handle where it can exert a bracing effect on the racket face against the impact of the ball. The thumb may be placed either across the back of the handle as shown in the photograph on page 27 or wrapped around the handle. My own method is to place it across, because I believe this position creates a more sensitive grip with slightly greater control over the racket face, but it is a matter of preference.

22

This grip is called the eastern backhand drive grip and it encourages the player to hit through the ball with the full face of the racket. At the same time it allows a certain amount of adaptability so that the ball can be played with underspin if necessary.

Some club players and juniors tend to develop underspin backhands mainly due to a slightly different position of the hand from the grip I have described. Underspin backhands have their value and weaknesses, and both are discussed in chapter 11. In general though I should stress that grips that bring the racket face open to and under the ball without the equal facility for allowing the racket face to hit through it, are limited in terms of higher standards of play.

As with the forehand grip, the forefinger should be spread slightly to encourage the arm and racket to be swung as one unit rather than as two units hinged at the wrist.

A number of players who try to change to the eastern backhand grip tell me that the ball tends to go into the net. This is because the natural tendency is for the wrist to allow the racket to turn over in the follow-through until it ends face downwards in the finish. In the flat or "lifted" drive try to keep the face of the racket vertical throughout the stroke. The wrist should be "locked" into the finish.

One of the commonest mistakes however is to overdue the bracing effect of the thumb by placing it *along* the handle. While this certainly stiffens up the wrist it prevents adaptability of the racket face for the low ball.

Changing from one grip to another during play is always a problem for the inexperienced player who feels there is insufficient time. A tip I have found most useful under these circumstances is for the player to await the service with the backhand grip when there is plenty of time to locate the fingers. If the ball then comes to the backhand side no grip change will be involved. Carry out this routine for a few weeks and suddenly you will discover that grip changing has come habitual for you.

Grips for the service and overhead smash

There is a bigger variation of grips for these strokes than for drives. This is because the demands of the beginner and the advanced player are quite different. Beginners for example sometimes experience the greatest difficulty in mastering the task of directing the ball into the correct service court. Advanced players on the other hand look upon the service stroke as their most effective attacking weapon and they develop the ability not only to hit the

24

ball hard, but also to spin the ball disconcertingly when they wish.

These two extremes of service need different grips. To make things as easy as possible for the beginner I strongly recommend using the same grip as for the forehand drive – the "shake-hands" grip. This allows the full face of the racket to be brought to the ball most easily. It has the additional advantage of keeping grip changing to a minimum. The advanced player however needs a grip which allows him from choice to hit hard or to produce spin and the most suitable grip for this is one that is extremely close to the *backhand* grip when the thumb is wrapped around the handle. By way of explanation however I should point out that in this case the face of the racket that is used for serving is the opposite one used for the backhand drive. The advantages of this grip for those who learn how to use it, are the wide adaptability it allows the player in angling the racket face to the ball and also the flexibility that it encourages. Quite unlike the drives, the service stroke demands a *throwing* action as it is gradually perfected.

So that in the case of a talented player who has first learned to serve with the forehand grip and later wants to move on to more advanced serving, a change of grip will be involved. This grip switch is fully dealt with in chapter 10.

25

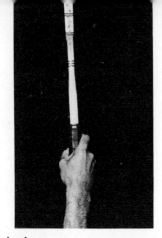

The Continental grip
The hand is positioned on top of the handle.

The player's grip for the overhead smash should match the one he uses for serving. If and when the change to an advanced serving grip is made, then the new grip should then be used for the overhead smash as well.

Grips for volleying

Knowing what problems many players experience in changing from one grip to another during play, I always recommend that they should learn to volley with the same grip as they use for the drives. The "shake-hands" grip is therefore recommended for the forehand volley and the eastern backhand grip for the backhand volley. This at least simplifies volleying development and allows the strokes to be built soundly and with firm execution.

26

As skill develops, players may find that in quick fire volleying exchanges near to the net, a one grip method for the volleys on both sides of the body is to be preferred. At such a time it may well be that the player has already made or is contemplating a change of grip for serving. If so then it is the new service grip that should be used for the one grip volleying technique. There are dangers in trying to master the one grip method too soon. This grip – the Continental – encourages wrist flexibility which I have pointed out is one of its advantages in serving. It can however lead to over-wristy volleying particularly on the

The Eastern backhand drive grip
The hand is a little further behind the racket than in the Continental grip, and the thumb locates itself across the back of the handle.

27

forehand side unless the stroke has first been well formed. Advanced players will almost certainly discover as they become more and more proficient, that they must be able to call on both the one-grip method and on their driving grips in learning to play the full range of low and high volleys in the most advantageous way.

Grips for the non-basic shots

I am a strong believer in simplifying the game as far as it is possible to do so. Where the ancillary shots like the drop shot, lob, and half-volley are concerned, use the grips you have already mastered. A forehand lob or drop shot should therefore be played with your forehand drive grip and vice versa the backhand side. The use of the grip for half-volleying will depend in nearly every case on which grip you are using for your volleying strokes.

How 'long' should you hold your racket?

To obtain maximum results from a racket you should hold it so that the fleshy part of your palm comes in contact with the end of the leather grip. To be able to do this and play with wrist control over the racket face, the racket must be of correct weight. Young players who find

28

their rackets too heavy when gripped in this position should slide the hand down the handle slightly. This however should be seen only as a temporary expedient. As soon as possible the racket should be held as I have described to provide you with its full power.

4 Develop a sound service action

There is no stroke in the game that is more important than the service. The beginner must first learn how to serve the ball into the correct part of the court to start the rally. For the club player a good or a bad service can mean all the difference between uninhibited enjoyment of the game or frustrated annoyance with one's shortcomings. For the tournament player a strong service is essential.

I am all in favour of starting off as quickly as possible to play the points and games even if it does mean using a simple push to propel the ball into the correct court. In this way the game is fun from the start. But I should also mention though that the game is a great deal more rewarding when you can serve the ball well. So players will be well advised to try and learn a sound action right from the start.

The standard of serving has never been higher in the game as a whole than it is today. This may be because its importance is more fully understood and possibly because it is the one stroke that can be practised without an opponent. There is however a world of difference between the simple flat service and the sophisticated racket work of the topspin service that takes several years to perfect. As with all

30

strokes a stage by stage build up is the most effective way of ending up with a powerful and accurate point-winning service stroke that can be such a boost to the player's all-round confidence.

The grip

The various grips are described in chapter 3. The "shake-hands" grip is the most suitable grip for beginners because it simplifies serving at the start. For advanced serving the Continental grip is the best one to use. It is almost identical to the eastern backhand grip. In serving, the thumb should be wrapped around the handle. The advanced serving grip is often called the "chopper" grip because when the racket is held in this way the player senses that it turns the edge of the frame towards the ball. The application of spin is therefore made easier with this grip but one important point to remember is to spread the forefinger slightly (photograph on page 26).

The stance and 'ready' position

The correct stance and a tidy "ready" position are the forerunners of consistent serving. One of the first things to be noted when watching first-class players is the careful way in which they place their feet and get ready for serving without any

31

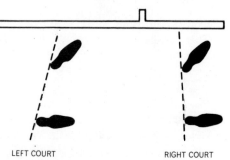

LEFT COURT   RIGHT COURT

Showing the different stance for serving to the left and right service courts. The positions shown relative to the centre mark are typical of those used in singles against a right-handed opponent.

trace of rushing. So this is the first thing to learn – to take your time.

The service is basically a *throwing* action and the stance should therefore be sideways. The shoulders are turned slightly to face the net with the racket extended forwards towards the opponent's service court (shown on page 33). One of the most common footfaults is to tread on the baseline when serving. I suggest you should place your front foot about four inches behind it

The service stance 'ready' position
Note the sideways position of the feet and their angles to the baseline. The racket is held out edge to the ground and pointing towards the service court. The balls are held in contact with the racket.

and learn to serve with your foot in that position until the ball has been struck. The front foot should point towards the right hand net post, with the back foot comfortably spaced – about shoulder width behind the left foot – and parallel to the baseline. Study figure on page 32 and note the different stance positions for serving to the right and left courts.

Your position along the baseline for

33

The 'ready' position for receiving the service and during play

The body is facing the net with the knees slightly bent for a quick movement in any direction. The racket is centrally positioned supported at the throat with the left hand. The head of the racket should be kept well up. The weight is fully forward and balance is being maintained for a quick recovery to the 'ready' position.

serving also varies according to whether you are playing doubles or singles and serving to a right- or left-handed player. For singles against right-handers stand about two feet to the right of the centre service mark on the baseline when serving into the first court, and about four or five

34

The backswing and footwork preparation for the forehand drive

The bodyweight is on the back foot. The left arm is fully extended towards the oncoming ball to assist balance as the racket is taken back.

feet to the left of the centre mark when serving to the second court. These positions should be reversed for play against left-handers. In doubles where you have a partner guarding part of the court, stand out a few feet wider towards each sideline when serving. The essential point to remember is that whether you are serving in singles or doubles, your position should

35

The forehand drive hitting position

The weight has gone forward onto the front foot, and the shoulders are turning into the shot. The left arm continues to aid balance.

take into account the possible angles of the return of service your opponent can make.

Holding the ball for serving

Learn to serve with two balls (never more) in your hand. The first ball to be used is held by the thumb and first two fingers, the second ball resting against the palm and held by the last two fingers. If the first ball is a fault, then the second ball is moved into the position that the first previously occupied.

36

Forehand drive finish

The right arm and racket continue to form an unbroken line with the racket face still vertical to the ground.

'Placing up' the ball for serving

The key to consistent serving lies in the accurate positioning of the service ball in the air. It must always be placed in the correct position relative to the server and in advanced serving it must also allow the player to use full height and reach to obtain full benefit from the stroke.

A greater degree of accuracy is obtained by thinking of the action as "placing" the ball, rather than throwing it, into the air. In

37

this connection a useful tip to remember is to keep the left wrist firm as the ball is launched upwards. A loose wrist action usually imparts finger spin to the ball and brings errors in its position.

To help beginners' co-ordination the ball should not be placed too high above the head. As skill and accuracy develop, the ball's height should gradually be increased to allow more time and room for the widening swing of the racket. When the service stroke has been fully developed the ball should be placed approximately twelve to eighteen inches *higher* than the server can reach with the racket and arm at full stretch. In this position it allows for a slowing down pause in the stroke before the upward moving racket face meets the falling ball to provide a reaction which imparts topspin in varying degrees according to the type of service being produced. More about this later.

The beginners' service

The degree of co-ordination that beginners possess varies so much, particularly with age, that I always suggest that players should first master the simplest of all overhead actions by raising the racket and ball together from the "ready" position and then pushing or patting the ball gently into the correct service court. Three points

38

must be watched at this early stage. They are firstly to keep your eye on the ball, secondly to place the ball correctly into the air, and thirdly to control the angle of the racket face as it meets the ball.

Once this simplest service form has been mastered – and the proof of this is the player's ability to direct at least seven out of every ten balls into the correct court – then a build-up of the service can begin.

Developing the swing

The *full* service swing should be mastered as soon as possible. Starting from the "ready" position both arms move *downwards* before they part, the left arm then moving upwards to place the ball into position while the right arm takes the racket upwards into the throwing action. By developing this action in easy stages the beginner can gradually feel his way into the full extent of the advanced service swing.

The service action

This is a combination of two actions – a *swing* of the racket from the shoulder followed by a wristy *throw* to strike the ball. By far the easiest way to understand the service stroke is to think of it as the ordinary throwing action in which the racket head is thrown *through* the ball. The

39

important part of it is the loop which the racket should make as it is taken down behind the player's head before it travels up to meet the ball with ever gathering speed.

Perhaps the best way of all to serve well is first to learn to throw a ball well. This is particularly important for girls who unlike boys almost never learn to throw in school games. Take a box of balls out on to court, throw them from the service "ready" position as far as possible, mark the distance of your best throw and then serve them back again. Week by week you will find your throwing power increasing and with it greater fluency with the service swing.

Balance

Look at the sequence pictures of the service and notice the way in which balance is maintained throughout the stroke. Control is more difficult if the player is falling off balance while serving. Three positions of balance must be observed in the building up of a sound service swing. The first – in the "ready" position, is simple. The second – during the pause position before the hit, is the crucial one. The third – immediately following the completion of the stroke, is the difficult one that tells the story of what has gone before.

40

Correct positioning of the service ball in the air is vital for correct balance. If the server finds himself continually falling away to one side or the other at the completion of the stroke, it is a sure sign that the ball is incorrectly placed. When the left arm is fully extended towards the ball and held there momentarily to counterbalance the right arm and racket action, it also aids accuracy in positioning the ball.

Rhythm

It should not be difficult for any keen player to develop sound rhythm with the service stroke. It is the one stroke which your opponent cannot affect. Not only that, but within reasonable limits you can choose your own time to serve. How surprising it is therefore to find that most beginners and many club players handicap their chances by rushing.

Learn to take plenty of time like the top players. They relax well and get themselves comfortably placed in the "ready" position first. You will often notice their habit of bouncing the ball before they go into the stroke. This is a drill to ensure that in the excitement of competition they do not hurry the action with the disastrous results which usually follow.

In terms of rhythm I like to think of the service as being in three parts. First comes

41

the lazy and relaxed wind-up which takes the racket up into the start of the throwing loop. Then follows the pause during which the racket is further slowed down while the server "collects" his weight and balance. Finally there is the lively whiplash action from the wrist to develop the tremendous racket head speed which provides the fierce power for speed or spin.

The follow-through and finish

There should be no holding back as the stroke is completed. Providing that you have correctly thrown your right shoulder forwards into the hitting action the racket will pass well to the left side of your body and arm. If you fail to get your right shoulder fully forwards there may be a painful ending – the racket can collide with your shins. Players seldom make this mistake more than once!

42

5 Develop power and control with your forehand drive

It is one of the peculiarities of lawn tennis that whereas the forehand drive is usually found to be the easiest stroke of all for beginners, it is certainly not seen in quite the same light by many first-class players. Beginners find it relatively simple to return the ball with the forehand because the racket can be swung clear of the body. Later on however as higher levels of play begin to demand more power from the stroke, the shoulders must be brought into use. This immediately introduces problems of footwork, and arm and body positioning.

If you are just beginning to play then I strongly recommend that you should learn to hold your racket for this stroke with the "shake-hands" grip. This grip is explained in chapter 3. Briefly it places the wrist and palm behind the handle where it can exert power and control. The spreading of the forefinger and to a lesser degree the second finger as well, is to encourage the development of a firm wristed swing *through* the ball instead of a "slap" at it from the wrist which can so easily come when the fingers are bunched together. "Wristiness" which often produces plenty of power but

not necessarily control, is usually a feature of the Continental grip in which the hand is placed on top of the handle. I do not recommend this grip for the forehand drive any more than I like the Western grip for it. This latter grip is obsolete in top class play these days but many beginners who start without coaching seem to pick up this grip. If you put your racket flat on the ground and then put your hand on the handle to pick it up again you will then have the Western grip. I mention it only out of interest and any beginner using this grip should make that change to an eastern "shake-hands" grip without delay.

This brings me to the question of changing your strokes in tennis. There are many established players who may find that their grips and stroke production differ from the methods I describe. I do not suggest for one moment that they should slavishly alter them before understanding some of the problems likely to be involved. These problems are explained in chapter 17 which is intended to answer the inevitable question "Should I change?" All I would say at this point is that although minor changes may often be accomplished with immediate benefit, major alterations are nearly always difficult to make, long drawn out, and fraught with danger.

44

Start from a tidy 'ready' position

Watch any player of class and you will see that after each stroke has been made, the racket and body are returned to a position shown on pages 34 and 54. Notice that this is a facing the net position with the knees slightly bent and the weight well forwards for a quick start in any direction. The racket is held well out from the body, supported at its "throat" with the left hand. Holding the racket well extended encourages you to give the ball plenty of room as you play it. A tucked-up "ready" position on the other hand tends to lead into a tucked-up stroke.

Supporting the racket with the left hand is also useful. Not only does it help to keep the head of the racket well up but it is a valuable aid in the rapid and accurate changing from one drive grip to the other. The importance of starting from and returning to a tidy "ready" position is that it allows the drives to originate from the same position each time the stroke is made – an essential part of the development of accurate and consistent stroke production.

The sideways hitting position

You might think that this is so obvious that it hardly need be mentioned. Far from it; the natural instinct of the beginner is to run straight at the ball. Then, the result is

45

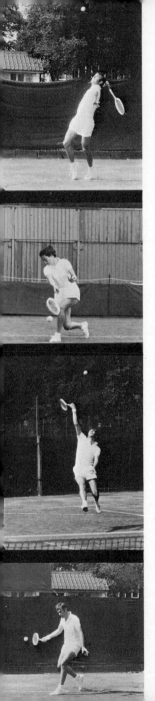

an upward push which sends it high into the air. If the ball is to be hit hard and kept in the court it must be given plenty of room as it approaches and then played from a sideways position. Look at the film sequence of the forehand drive. If you can master the footwork to bring your body into the sideways position, then the correct impact position for a player using the "shake-hands" grip is opposite the front knee. The striking position will be a few inches further back for the player using a Continental grip.

Footwork

The success or failure of virtually every stroke depends on the footwork for it. The chances of making successful shots are considerably reduced with bad footwork. So the player should look upon sound footwork as the foundation on which everything else is built.

I have found that it is unwise for the average player to become too involved in footwork theory. Providing that the basic footwork pattern can be mastered in pivoting sideways from the "ready" position then further development can proceed without too much difficulty.

The basic movement

The correct footwork and swing of the

46

racket - and the important co-ordination and timing of one with the other - can best be mastered by breaking the stroke down into a stage by stage development. From the facing-the-net "ready" position shown on pages 34 and 54 make the turn-and-step-forwards footwork to finish in the balanced position shown in the photograph on page 37. When this has become familiar, stand in the same sideways position and make the correctly shaped forehand drive swing. Then put both movements together trying to co-ordinate the footwork and racket swing to produce a flowing and rhythmical movement.

Do this first of all without the ball. Familiarity with the footwork and racket work soon follows and when it does, the easiest moving ball – one that can be dropped out of the left hand – can be introduced. As you turn your shoulders at the start of the basic movement, extend your left arm fully and drop the ball in a position that will allow you to make the full co-ordinated action of feet and racket while hitting the ball and then holding the *correctly balanced finish*. An incorrectly positioned ball will cause a loss of balance.

The advantages of building up the stroke in this way should be obvious. First it allows the player to build up sound form without the distraction of a moving ball. When the swing and footwork start

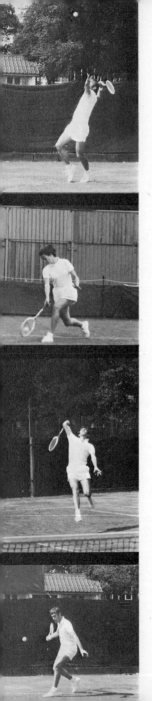

to become habitual the ball can be introduced. Once these simple dropped balls can be hit on balance to any part of the court, it is only a matter of time and experience before the entire movement will start to reproduce itself during play. Progress will be even faster if the development of the stroke from the basic movement is assisted first by having someone throw a few dozen well placed balls so that you can practise unsticking the feet with a small up-on-the-toes skip out of the static position from which you have built up the stroke. When the ball is wide and a number of steps are needed to reach it, try to ensure that you arrive in position ahead of the ball so that a balance-gathering pause can be made on the *back* foot before the step-in and stroke are made.

Learn the looped swing

A quick examination of the forehand drive sequence pictures will show you what is meant by a looped swing. Instead of being taken back and brought forwards on a straight line, the racket describes a slightly looped path, moving upwards out of the "ready" position and then after dropping down to the bottom of the back-swing loop, moving upwards as it is brought forwards to meet the ball. The

48

resulting impact imparts slight topspin to the ball to improve the player's control and margin for error.

Control with the wrist

Many players make the mistake of trying to produce power from the wrist whereas its basic function is to *control* the drive. A firm wrist at impact will prevent the racket face "giving" too much or twisting under the stress of a ball struck slightly off centre. This does not mean to say that the wrist must never be used in playing the forehand drive. Under the pressure of competition, compromises must continually be made and the wrist provides the final adjustment to the racket face that this necessitates. Try to appreciate however that the less the wrist needs to work as a corrector of footwork and body positioning errors the more consistent the stroke is likely to become. The head of the racket should be kept well up throughout the stroke.

Playing the high and low balls

It is a mistake to think that all balls can be hit equally hard. The high ball for example played from near to the baseline is more difficult to hit with power than the waist high return. For one thing the wrist control

49

is more difficult higher up, and power is less easy to develop. The high forehand drive needs a higher take back of the racket and players should be careful not to try to do too much with a return which may look easy but is often quite the opposite.

Providing that the low ball is being played from close to your baseline it can be hit hard with the lifted drive I have described. The secret of controlling it is to keep the head of the racket well up by bending at the knees to lower the stroke to the ball. Do not stoop. If you keep your back straight balance is more easily maintained.

Hitting 'round the outside'

Any forehand drive in which the racket face is dragged across the ball will carry sidespin and depart from a straight line of flight. This allows the ball to drift out over the sideline and it will deprive the player of the full width of the court for a down-the-line passing shot. Hitting "round the outside" is the player's conscious effort to avoid slice and to hit the ball cleanly. The technique demands strength of wrist, perfect footwork to bring the body and ball into the correct sideways hitting position, and a well executed body pivot as the stroke is played.

The follow-through and finish

Ball control is developed from the moment the ball meets the racket until it leaves the strings. Playing the ball from the shoulder allows a slower stroke than when the ball is "wristed". The forward-moving body-weight ensures plenty of power and the result is that the ball is kept longer on the strings. This control can be developed further by keeping the arm straight in the finish instead of pulling the strings off the ball early by allowing the elbow to bend. This point is clearly shown in the film sequence of Newcombe.

Playing the short forehand drive

This shot which often presents itself as a set-up is frequently missed by juniors and club players. There are two common errors that players make in returning this ball. First is the natural inclination of the inexperienced player to run straight to the ball – and crowding it as a result. The second is a more general failure to get up to the ball. It must then be played too far in front of the body and out it goes over the baseline. The correct procedure is to move quickly to get up to the ball early in its bounce, and once there to turn and make the usual balance-gathering pause before playing the ball from the normal sideways position.

51

6 Learn the modern attacking backhand drive

The backhand drive always gives beginners a lot of trouble and many club players too find themselves handicapped by a lack of power and control with this stroke. Those who experience nothing but difficulty should be reassured by the fact that among tournament players there are more really good backhand drives to be seen than forehands – surely the proof that once the initial problems with the backhand have been mastered it is the easier of the two strokes to develop.

Where do the difficulties come in backhand play? Mainly I would say in the use of unsound grips and the failure of many players to get the right foot across to allow the shoulders to turn fully for the wind-up. Once the player masters these basic points he will not only enjoy hitting the ball off this wing but he will find a remarkable amount of power can be developed with the stroke.

Use a sound grip

The eastern backhand grip or the Continental grip which do not differ greatly are suitable for the backhand drive. Both are described in chapter 3. My personal preference is for the former because it encourages an extremely firm wrist and the development of a lifted drive with the slight topspin which can be such an effective defence for your passing shots against the volleyer. Both grips allow underspin to be used when necessary but I always emphasise to pupils with high ambitions that too much use of underspin on the backhand will quickly choke the development of a modern attacking drive played with a touch of "lift".

Remember that whichever grip you use, spread your forefinger slightly away from your second, and leave a rather smaller gap between your second and third fingers. This aids control and helps you to swing the racket as an extension of your arm. Players who are used to gripping the racket with their fingers bunched together usually tell me that spreading them results in a feeling of restriction. You will never achieve consistent results if you try to "wrist" the ball with a table tennis-like flick. The modern backhand should be played with a locked wrist. The spreading of the fingers is an aid in *control* over power which must come from the back and shoulders.

The 'one piece' wind-up

Once your grip is sound build up your

53

The 'ready' position for receiving the service and during play

The body is facing the net with the knees slightly bent for a quick movement in any direction. The racket is centrally positioned supported at the throat with the left hand. The head of the racket should be kept well up. The weight is fully forward and balance is being maintained for a quick recovery to the 'ready' position.

stroke from the "ready" position. Hold the racket well out in front of your body supported at its "throat" with the left hand. Keep your right arm and the racket in an unbroken line (photograph on page 55).

It is vital to appreciate that the ball must be met at the side of the body. The most

The backswing and footwork preparation for the backhand drive

The weight is on the back foot as the racket is taken back supported by the left hand. This allows the shoulders to turn fully. The wrist is locked.

common error with beginners is in failing to turn. They allow the ball to approach too close to the body and the result is a push at it from the front instead of a properly executed swing.

If you learn to take the racket into the wind-up with a "one-piece" backswing you will avoid pushing at the ball and a sound stroke will develop with practice. From the facing-the-net "ready" position the entire unit of shoulders, arms and

55

Backhand drive hitting position
The weight has gone forwards on to the front foot as the ball is met opposite the front knee. The head of the racket is kept well up at this stage and the left arm is now aiding balance.

racket is turned from the hips to take the racket into the backswing. Up to this stage there is no independent movement of the racket, wrist or arms. A further wind-up for the stroke is then made by continuing the shoulder turn to take the racket into the full extent of the backswing with the left hand still guiding and controlling it. With the shoulders now well round, the player will be looking back over the right shoulder for the approaching ball. Due to the extent of the wind-up the ball can only

Backhand drive finish

The arm and racket form an unbroken line during the follow-through. The weight has gone fully forwards and good balance will enable the player to return quickly to the original 'ready' position.

be seen out of the corner of the eyes.

Use of the left arm

In the modern backhand drive the left arm is used more than previously. It should not be allowed to go for a ride on the racket; it is there for a purpose. Keeping it on the racket into the backswing ensures that the shoulders are cleared well out of the way for the stroke. It can also be used positively

57

to guide and control the path of the racket to produce a more accurate backswing. Once the stroke has been made, the racket should be returned back again into the original "ready" position where the left hand once again supports it and allows the right wrist to relax.

Although beginners who learn this method find little difficulty in developing it, there may be a feeling of restriction for established players who try to master it, particularly when playing the ball on the run. Experience has shown me however that with perseverance players quickly gain ease and fluency with the method which then brings them a feeling of great solidarity with their swing.

The sideways hitting position

Once the player has learned to turn the shoulders fully, the way is clear for the ball to be played from the side so that it can be firmly struck without flying high into the air. The point of impact is approximately opposite the front knee. Due to the different footwork that is needed for the lifted and underspin drives however, the player may gain the impression that the correct impact position for the underspin backhand is much further back than for the lifted drive. It all depends on how the feet are placed.

58

Footwork

If the player concentrates on moving to the ball so that it can come to the side of his body, it will encourage him to get the right foot across. Without this correct movement of the right foot it will be impossible for the shoulder turn and correct backswing to be made. I have sometimes overcome pupils' initial reluctance to turn fully for the backhand by asking them to use their imagination and to think how they would fling the racket over to their opponent's court from the backhand side of the body. The backhand drive demands the same full shoulder wind-up and movement of the feet.

The basis of consistent play is consistent footwork. When the placing of the feet is erratic, adaptations of the stroke and shoulder and wrist actions become necessary and control becomes elusive. As the player grows aware of the way that the swing can be "grooved" when the footwork is mastered the development of a sound and reliable stroke becomes only a matter of practice.

The feet however need to be placed differently for the lifted drive and the underspin shot. When the shoulder turn is beings mastered the natural inclination will be for the right foot to step *across*. This is correct only when the ball is to be

59

played back with underspin. For the lifted drive the foot should be placed *forwards*. In this position it provides a solid platform for the heavier impact of the flat struck ball.

Much of the success in developing a backhand drive of real class depends also on the co-ordination between the footwork and racket swing. As a means of providing some indication of the timing required, I suggest that you learn to turn on the left foot as the ball comes towards you and then to tumble the bodyweight forwards *alongside* the ball as the stroke is made. The right foot should be on the ground a fraction of a second before the ball is struck. It is a common error with beginners to get the right foot down too early.

The basic movement

The best possible way of building up correct footwork and sound stroke-form is by the simple stage by stage development that has already been described for the forehand drive. The player first masters the correct movements of the feet, shoulders, arms and racket swing without a ball. When this "shadow swinging" has become fluent and the various actions well coordinated then introduce the easiest moving ball – one out of the player's hand.

60

With a little practice it can be tossed gently into the air to bounce in the correct position for this next stage of the stroke's development. The true test of how well you are mastering the backhand at this point is whether you can begin to direct the ball first into one corner of the court opposite and then into the other.

It is of course a big jump from hitting a dropped ball out of your hand to returning those sent to you in a game. To bridge this gap you should try to join forces with another keen player and help one another by carefully tossing balls to each other's backhand side for practising the stroke against simple moving balls.

I cannot stress enough the importance of learning to balance yourself throughout the backhand drive. A correctly balanced finish whether for the "shadow swing", the stroke with the dropped ball, or when driving in a game, puts the weight onto the front foot with the back foot "toeing" the ground as the finish is held momentarily before the return to the "ready" position for the next stroke. A disciplined finish with perfect balance when hitting a dropped ball is also important in teaching the player the correct distance the ball should be from the body. Getting it either too close or too far away will immediately destroy a balanced finish.

61

Shape of the swing

The backswing may be straight but I prefer it to be slightly looped in shape. Not only does this produce a more fluent stroke but a variety of shots can be disguised more readily. The full loop for example will be made for the lifted drive preparation. The same start will be made for the underspin shot which can be hidden from the opponent until the racket is brought forwards and down to the ball from the top of the backswing. From this latter preparation too the underspin drop shot can be produced with disguise.

Action of the wrist

There is a considerable strain put on the wrist in a well executed backhand drive. As in the forehand stroke, the wrist must prevent the racket face from sagging under the weight of the ball at impact. If it fails to do this then the result will be a deflected shot to the left of the intended direction. Whether you are hitting through the ball with a lifted drive or coming slightly under the ball with deliberate backspin, the wrist must *control* the ball at impact and avoid the common error of the ball being allowed to control the wrist.

The follow-through and finish

The construction of the arm enables the

desirable straight line of the racket and arm to be maintained more easily in the follow-through to the backhand drive than in the forehand stroke. There are however two common errors which show themselves at this stage of the stroke, The first is a tendency of the wrist to "give up" and allow the racket face to roll over, and the second is for the racket to wander off to the right of the ball's line of flight.

The solidarity of the arm, wrist and racket, must not be relaxed until the full extent of the follow-through has been reached. By concentrating on this point greater control over the direction of the finish can be exerted. The aim should be to keep the racket strings in contact with the ball for as long as possible. Forward moving bodyweight that is correctly balanced allows the player to lengthen this "control period".

7 Receiving and returning the service

There is plenty of proof that the service stroke governs competitive play at the medium and higher levels. Longer and longer service-dominated sets have for example brought the "tie-breaker" to top tennis – a method of bringing the set to an end after an agreed number of games-all have been reached. But although every player must learn to serve well, one of the best ways to combat the effectiveness of opponents' services is to develop the skill to return them consistently and accurately.

There is more to this than simply watching the ball well and then taking a careful swing at it. To start with you must be able to "read" an opponent's service well. What type of service is coming to you? Is it likely to be fast or slow? Is it carrying spin and if so what type of spin? The correct answers to these questions flash to the aid of a skilful returner of the service like Australia's Ken Rosewall. The player must also get to know all about the bounce-behaviour of the ball from the various types of service and on different court surfaces. On grass for example a slice service slides through on bouncing and continues to swerve. On hard courts with their rougher surface, spin is checked during the bounce and some or all of the swerving effect is lost. This sort of knowledge is gained through experience but right from the beginner level certain basic rules should be observed.

Where to stand

Most beginners stand much too close to the service line to receive the ball. This is encouraged by the soft services of their beginner-opponents. But the moment they meet a player who can serve the ball harder and deeper they are in trouble. So if you know your opponent can serve the ball fairly fast, stand well back near the baseline, but be ready to spot the softer and shorter service as soon as it leaves the racket.

In general therefore the receiver should stand a few feet further back – but never more than two or three feet behind the baseline – for the first service. Then if it is a fault, the second ball can be awaited from closer in.

It is a mistake to leave one side of your service court more open than the other. By trying to shield a weak backhand by standing well over on that side, you present a wide open target on the forehand for the server. It also prevents your backhand return from gaining strength. It is far better in the long run to stand in a more

65

central position and learn how to return the ball from the backhand side. In any case as you play against better servers, their accuracy will give you no alternative.

Be alert in the 'ready' position

The "ready" position has already been adequately covered. It is however vital for the receiver to be concentrating fully as the serve comes down. In top class play where the ball is served at over 100 m.p.h. the receiver has less than half a second to sight the ball, move and play the return. At every level of play alertness in receiving the service is the vital aspect of success. I must again mention that for those beginners who have not gained fluency with grip changing, the return of service should be awaited with the grip to which they find it the more difficult to change.

Develop the skip start

Watch tournament players receiving service and you will notice that as the server makes contact with the ball, they skip up on to their toes to "unstick" their feet. The timing of it is important to allow the receiver to move quickly in any direction. This skip start must be mastered as a habit by all players.

Get the return back into court

The player who seldom fails to put the return of service back into court is always a difficult person to play. Avoid over-ambitious slogging at the ball. The occasional flashy winner will not compensate for the inevitable errors. Remember it is not essential to win the point outright with the return of service. A sound return consistently played back into court will usually bring a much better percentage of points.

Neither should it be forgotten that where the server is following the service to the net and volleying, the return which he must then make is never easy when played on the run. Under this type of serving pressure there is a tendency for the receiver to take his eyes off the ball. This temptation to look up to watch the server must be resisted. Of all occasions when the ball must be most carefully watched, none is more important than during the return of service.

Keep the server guessing

Even a consistent return will lose its effect if it is never varied. An occasional lobbed reply is a useful answer to the net-rushing server. Soft and short services should be attacked carefully. Fast services though are usually controlled with greater ease by

67

"blocking" them back into court with a volley-type action. When the server remains on the baseline after serving, then the return should be made as deep as possible. A good length return however to the server who volleys your reply, is one that is played shorter, either wide or down to his feet as he moves forwards.

When you are faced with returning a topspin service that "kicks" up high to your backhand, it is sometimes better to take it on the rise after it bounces and to block it firmly. In world class tennis, players like Rod Laver, Tony Roche and Arthur Ashe, have mastered the topspin return of service from the backhand side. This is an extremely difficult stroke to play well and the less difficult sliced backhand return should be perfected first.

In doubles play where all four players are usually engaged in a race to get into the close-in volleying position at the net, the return of service must be kept low or it will be murdered. The server's partner at the net is always a constant threat to the receiver with possible interceptions. It is sometimes worth while to return the ball down his sideline. Even if he does not move across then, you will have clearly indicated that you may do so again at any time. In this way your return of service can continually threaten him.

Under heavy serving pressure in doubles

the lob is of the utmost value. Hit it firmly and as deep as possible, making sure that it is not so low that your own partner has insufficient time to move into the best defensive position. In mixed doubles one of the most effective returns of the girl's service when her partner is at the net ready to intercept, is the deep cross-court lob.

8 Develop your attack with sound volleying

It is surprising to find how many players there are who look upon volleying as some sort of superior skill that is beyond them. Nothing could be further from the truth. Some players certainly possess the quick eye which really good volleying requires and may take to it more readily than others. But there is no reason why all players should not be able to develop an ability to play the ball before it bounces providing they tackle it in the right way and then persevere with their practice.

I hardly need to stress how important volleying is for players who hope to do well in competition. It increases the player's range of tactics, allows him to use greater resource during play and of course is the winning way of playing in the higher levels of matchplay.

I have sometimes seen it suggested that the best way to learn how to volley is by forcing yourself to move forwards to the net and that growing skill will follow as the ball is shot at you. This is rather like suggesting to a non-swimmer that the way to learn how to swim is to jump in at the deep end and have a go. There are more effective

70

and less alarming ways of learning both skills! The advice however touches on one side of volleying that must be learnt, namely to play from well inside the service court. When volleys are made eight to ten feet from the net they can more often than not be hit *downwards* into the opponent's court. They become progressively more difficult to play successfully the further back the volleyer stands. Coaching experience however has shown me that confidence must come first and that this soon encourages the player to stand closer to the net.

Growing confidence comes as the various strokes can be played more effectively. It also grows – particularly in the case of young players – when the fear of being hit by the ball begins to vanish as the player's eye becomes sharper. Let us start with a stage by stage build-up of the volleys.

First the player must appreciate that volleying and driving are different actions. In chapter 2 I emphasized that whereas the drives should be thought of as *swings*, the volleys are *pushes* through the ball. When the ball is higher up but below the required height for an overhead smash, the volleys can be thought of as *punches* through the ball. Compare the pictures of the forehand and backhand drives and volleys to appreciate these basic differences in the actions.

71

The grips

For beginners I recommend that the normal driving grips should be used when learning to volley. This involves grip changing but gives the player the advantage of using familiar grips while learning unfamiliar shots. For advanced play a one-grip method is preferable because it allows the ball to be returned more easily during quick-fire exchanges. This grip should be the same as the service grip, the fingers being spread as usual. I suggest that players who learn to volley with their normal driving grips should not make the change to the one-grip technique until they are ready to change also to this grip for serving. They will then be able to use a single grip for serving, volleying and smashing.

The forehand volley

An alert "ready" position as previously described is essential. It is also desirable to bend rather lower when awaiting the volleys than when driving from the back of the court. Hold the racket with your *backhand* volley grip – it is easier to cover your body with the racket if the ball is hit straight at you.

It must become instinctive for the volleyer to initiate each stroke with a shoulder turn. The footwork, when the ball

72

is wide and you have to stretch to reach it, is similar to the forehand drive footwork. In other words get the left foot forwards or across as the ball demands. When the ball is directed straight at you and you do not have time to move your feet then sway from the hips, turning your shoulders into the sideways position from which the volley can be controlled. Balance and weight control are important if quick recoveries are to be made under pressure. As in driving, play the volleys with your weight moving forwards on to the front foot. At all times keep on your toes.

Imagine for a moment how you would catch a ball in your hand. You would simply place the palm, slightly opened to receive the falling ball and there would be little movement of your hand. The same preparation with an absence of backswing should be observed in learning to play the volleys. From the "ready" position simply turn the shoulders, do not take the racket any further back, and then play the ball with a firm-wristed push.

Control is gained during the follow-through when the ball should be held in contact with the racket strings for as long as possible. The low volleys depend on control more than speed and this can be further developed by the use of slight underspin. It has the effect of giving the volleyer extra "touch" as the ball slides

73

across the strings. Be careful not to apply this underspin by *cutting* the ball. The correct action is best described as *blocking* the ball back with underspin. Obviously the degree to which you open or close the racket face in volleying depends on the position of the ball in relation to the net. Above shoulder level the volleys should be played with a flat racket face. The wrist should also be kept quite firm on the forehand volleys that are above head height. You should only switch into the overhead smash when the ball's height gives you both the extra room for the flexibly wristed stroke, and also the time to make it.

Keep your back straight and learn to bend from your knees when playing the low volleys. Balance is then made much easier.

The backhand volley

Although this stroke differs from the backhand drive, the development of the backhand volley is usually governed by the player's mastery of the drive. The reason is that the same shoulder-turn must be made for both to be played well. If the player keeps his body facing the net when playing the backhand volley, then just as in driving, the ball is likely to sail high into the air. This shoulder-turn is made more easily when the right foot is advanced during the

74

stroke but as I mentioned earlier there are many occasions in volleying when the ball allows insufficient time for the ideal placing of the feet. At such times – usually when the ball is coming straight at you – develop the habit of swaying the body sideways from your hips to produce the necessary turn of the shoulders.

Again try to see a mental picture of the correct action you are trying to make in playing the backhand volley. This time it is rather like catching the ball on the back of the outstretched hand. The racket face is no more than a big hand that should be well controlled at impact by "locking" the wrist through the stroke.

I have already dealt with the grip and the "ready" position from which the stroke should originate. The beginner will have to fight against taking the racket back too far – a habit which comes from the drive preparation. As in the forehand volley, the backhand volley should be met slightly forwards of the sideways position. As a guide think of the impact position as being opposite the front (right) foot. This of course is assuming that your feet are ideally placed.

Play the lower balls with underspin for the increased control it can give and which these balls need. Many players make the mistake of "giving up" with the wrist as they slide the racket face under the ball at

impact. Keeping the wrist "locked" right through to the finish puts quite a strain on the wrist and arm muscles. Practise "shadow swinging" for the backhand volley keeping the racket head above wrist level from start to finish. The proof of a correct action is if you tire your muscles after half a dozen! Practise playing imaginary low volleys by bending at your knees while keeping the back straight for easier balance. The high backhand volley is difficult to play with consistent accuracy but like the volley on the forehand side must be played with a solid wrist and a flat racket face. Only when the ball is too high to reach without jumping should the wrist flex for the backhand smash which is described in chapter 9.

Correct use of the volleys

Many players try to do too much with the ball when they volley. Think first in terms of controlling the ball and its direction, and later in hitting harder. Three of the four types of volleys you can use depend purely on control. They are the short angled volleys, stop-volleys and lob-volleys. The fourth type – the deep volley – needs both control and speed to be effective.

Angled volleys are produced as one might expect, by angling the racket face to deflect the ball sharply from its line of

76

flight. The stop-volley aims to win the point by stopping the ball short just over the net. Keep your wrist firm on this delicate shot, "cushioning" the ball against the strings as you take the speed off it. Do not try to play this shot when too far from the net. The lob-volley is, as its name implies, a volley that scores by being lobbed over the opponent's head when he is close in at the net. Keep your eye on this one. It needs a really fine degree of control. Hit too hard and it will go out of court; too short a lob-volley will be eaten up by the opponent. Perfect deep volleying first then angled volleying, adding the other types to your repertoire later.

Above all practise regularly. Use a wall to try and keep the rally going or practise with another keen player. See how many volleys you can make before the ball bounces on the ground and continually strive to increase the number.

Photographs of the volleys
are on pages 124–127

77

9 Learn to smash with confidence

The overhead smash is the most spectacular shot in tennis and when played successfully is one of the most satisfying. It can bring a feeling of rising confidence to the attacking player whose entire net game depends on its effectiveness.

Two courses of action are open to the baseliner when you move forwards into the attack. He can go for the passing shot or he can lob the ball high in the air to try and drive you back. If you can smash away the lob for a winner then you discourage him from lobbing too much. At the same time your confidence in being able to deal successfully with lobs encourages you to play closer to the net, from which position your volleys will also be more effective against the passing shots your opponent will be forced to make. And so your whole attacking game is given a sharper edge.

If on the other hand your smash is weak then you handicap your attack by it. Your opponent will keep lobbing and gradually you will drop further and further back until you become vulnerable to the passing shot as well.

The smash is of course a stroke played when the ball is high above the player's

78

head, and therefore it is closely related to the service.

There is little point in beginners trying to master the smash until they have first developed co-ordination, fluency and control over the service stroke. The overhead smash is more difficult because it must be played against a faster falling ball that is often awkwardly placed and needs skilful footwork to bring the player into the correct position for it. When the service is coming along satisfactorily then attempts to develop the overhead smash will be more successful.

The grip should be the same for both strokes. If, as your game improves, you decide to change to an advanced serving grip, then you must also change your grip for the smash at the same time.

As in serving, the player should think of the overhead smash as a "throwing" action. The wrist should be strongly flexible as the ball is played. The timing needs to be precise and therefore the footwork must be nimble. Remember the cardinal rule in preparing for the stroke. It is that the instant the lob goes up turn sideways towards it and then move in this position to bring the ball within reach. Many lobs that have to be smashed are deep and the player must move backwards to reach them. While doing this the body should be kept in the sideways position

with the left foot crossing over in front of the right foot in a series of ryhthmical skip steps. This can be seen in the film sequence of the stroke. There are occasions of course when the lob is so high that its speed in falling makes timing too difficult. Lobs of this height should be allowed to bounce and then be dealt with. Only experience will teach you which lobs to take before they bounce and which ones you should bounce-smash.

Whenever possible it is better to play the overhead smash with your feet kept in contact with the ground. There are times though, when for example you are caught close in at the net with a deep lob, when a jump smash is the only way to reach the ball. It is spectacular, exhilarating, but difficult to master the intricate co-ordination of footwork and timing.

Learn the smash in the same stage by stage build-up as for the other strokes. First perfect your serve until your timing and control over it are consistent. Then find someone to play some high lobs to you in the middle of the court. Let these bounce and then get used to smashing them away. Position yourself each time so that the ball is brought into the same place above your head as in serving. From this stage advance to the smashing of lobs well in front of you and within easy reach. Do not try to hit too hard. Develop your sense of timing first. Later you can start hitting deeper lobs and then finally learn how to jump for those that would otherwise be out of reach.

The racket action is not quite the same as in serving, It differs in that the wind-up for the smash should be more restricted than for the service stroke. Study the difference by referring to the sequence pictures of both strokes. Since the successful smash depends mainly on speed rather than on precise placing, the ball should be struck with a flat racket face or with very little spin. There is a tendency for many players to try and hit too hard. Control the ball by keeping a little of your power in reserve.

One of the most common errors made by players in overhead smashing is their failure to use the left arm properly. As the right arm takes the racket back into the wind-up, the left arm should be extended stiff and straight towards the falling ball. This "pointing" of the arm aids balance and helps to keep the shoulders well turned until the stroke is made. The left arm is then brought down just as in serving to assist balance in the finish.

The overhead smash is a confidence shot. Once you have decided whether to play the ball either before or after bouncing, then go for it with no thought of whether you might miss.

81

The backhand smash

When a lob is directed deep over your backhand shoulder the only way of returning the ball may be with a backhand smash – the most difficult stroke in the game to play with control and consistency. Top players try to move round a high lob on the backhand side to play it with the overhead smash because the return can then be played with much more power. There are occasions however, when a clever opponent forces you to use the backhand smash.

The differences between this stroke and the high backhand volley should be remembered. The high backhand volley which has already been dealt with in chapter 8, is played with the feet firmly on the ground and with the wrist kept locked throughout. The backhand smash is employed on a higher ball which can only be reached by jumping. In this position the wrist must be kept flexible while the shot is played. The action is perhaps best described as a strong wrist "flick".

The great difficulty with this shot is to control the angle of the racket face. Few players have the requisite strength and co-ordination and sense of timing that are needed to play the backhand smash really well. Your own limitations with this stroke are certainly the best recommendation for

82

trying to force your opponent to play this shot.

By all means practise backhand smashing. Try to place the ball back deep to your opponent's weakness. You will find this to be more effective than trying to win by speed alone.

10 Learning a spin service

The build-up of a sound swing should be the first consideration as soon as the player has started to serve the ball into court. Once the mechanics of the stroke and its rhythm and timing have been mastered the player should be capable of serving the ball at a useful speed. The next stage in the more efficient use of the service is the development of more control and greater effect.

If the forehand "shake-hands" grip has been used so far in serving then a change must now be made for two reasons. By altering the position of the hand on to the top of the handle (see chapter 3 for details) the wrist is in a position where its flexibility can be used to the full. It also brings the racket face to the ball at an angle and in this position spin can be imparted more easily.

The reason why spin should be used in advanced serving will be discussed in chapter 11. It is difficult for many players making their first attempts at the spin service to accept the idea that spin on the ball can make the service easier. The problems involved make many give up the idea of learning spin and they return to their safe flat-hit stroke preferring to accept its limitations.

84

Although I have known cases where talented boys have been able to master the spin service in a shorter time, the learning period for most players is several years. It is one thing to be able to spin the service ball correctly, but quite a different degree of skill must be acquired to direct the ball to any part of the court.

I mention this not to discourage ambitious players but only to put the mastery of the stroke in correct perspective.

Learn the sidespin service first

This is the easier of the two types of service spin to learn. The ball is struck a glancing blow with the racket face moving from left to right. The first task is to direct the spinning ball towards the court. In the majority of cases players will find it has been deflected too far to the left.

The server must appreciate that in making any spin service, the path of the racket to the ball must be angled to the right of its intended direction. In other words the shoulders must turn much more to get the back well round so that the correct swing can be made. For all players who have been used to hitting flat services, the initial sensation will be that a false aiming point far to the right must be selected if the spinning ball is to go into court. Once the strangeness of an altered

85

service swing has been overcome, the sidespin service can be developed without too much trouble.

The position of the ball in the air for this service should be a little further back and slightly to the right of the position for the flat service and the ball must be struck when it is a few inches below full height and reach. It gives a sideways swerving flight to the ball through the air and when under full control it can be swung out wide of the player or else be made to move into his body to cramp his return. The sidespin service is not so physically tiring as the topspin variety and I recommend players to master it first.

The topspin service

When you watch top class players you will almost certainly see them using topspin on their second service balls. The reason will be clear if you watch the ball carefully. It dips sharply during flight and "kicks" awkwardly on bouncing. So it gives the server added safety and is never an easy return for the receiver.

The spin is really a combination of topspin and sidespin. If you can imagine the ball having a clock face then the racket strings should strike the ball a glancing blow from seven to one o'clock. For this the ball must be placed a little further to

86

the left and not too far forward. The shoulders must turn just as in the slice service and the extent of the turn controls the angle of the swing to the ball and the amount of spin that can be applied.

One big difference between the slice and topspin services though is that the back must be arched and the knees bent for balance during the topspin service. The impression the player should gain is that when the ball has been placed in the air, he must turn and bend under it. Although the follow-through in the American Twist – which is an exaggerated topspin service – ends to the right side of the player, the finish of the normal topspin service should be to the left side of the body. In this position it allows the right shoulder to come forwards to provide momentum for the more rapid move forwards to volley the receiver's return.

It must be appreciated though that a topspin service that cannot be directed accurately is usually easy meat for the opposition. Its high bounce makes it vulnerable to a powerful forehand.

Again the stroke should be learned in easy stages. First master the sliced service. Then gradually bring the ball into a position further to the left which will allow the racket to be brushed slightly upwards as it meets the ball. Later on as familiarity with the action develops, more spin can be

applied. The player learning this type of service must be prepared to see its development over several seasons of play. The precision and accuracy required when using the racket face angled in this way is far more demanding than in other types of service.

The need for racket head speed

To be used successfully the strings must meet the ball at high speed if sufficient spin is to be developed to produce the bigger safety margin of a dipping flight. In the learning stages and particularly during matchplay, the player will sometimes feel that he must ease up in serving the ball in this way to make sure it goes in. Then, because the racket is moving more slowly, a great deal of spin is lost, and it loses the curving flight which is its safety margin.

I must emphasize strongly that any player who wants to learn to serve with topspin must have the courage to *attack* the ball with fast racket head speed. There will be double faults galore at the start. These are the cost of attempting a difficult stroke which when fully mastered brings extra confidence to the player who then knows he can serve his *second* ball offensively.

88

11 Make spin work for you

Correctly used, spin on the ball can be of great value, but it can also be abused if its purposes are not understood. There are two advantages it can bring. First it can help the player's control of the ball to produce more effective returns, and second it can be used to make things more difficult for the opponent.

The effects of four types of spin must be appreciated before they can be used advantageously. Topspin is of great value in attack because its dipping trajectory through the air allows the ball to be hit harder and still fall within the lines of the court. Underspin flattens out the ball's flight and by holding it longer in the air allows the player more time for court coverage. It is therefore mainly for defensive purposes although it can also be used under certain circumstances for attacking manoeuvres. By combining these two types of spin, mixed effects can be produced. For example with half topspin and half sidespin, a dipping and swerving flight can be given to the ball. Where underspin and sidespin are combined, slice is produced which gives a floating and sideways swerve to the ball.

The flight of the ball is altered by spin due to the effect of the air meeting its cover. When the balls are new and fresh from the

89

box they take spin rather less than when they start to fluff up after a few games have been played. Later on as they become worn and smooth, the effect of spin is again reduced and the balls feel "light" off the racket. So it is important to appreciate the state of the balls you are using at any particular time.

Spin however is part of more advanced play and beginners should not involve themselves in its intricacies while their basic strokes are in the formative stage. First master the technique of bringing the full face of the racket to the ball before experimenting with closing and opening the racket face to produce the glancing blow which imparts spin.

Use of topspin

Slight topspin can improve performance once a sound outline of the forehand and backhand drives is developing. It allows the ball to be hit harder and higher over the net than with the flat hit return. For most players it is easier to learn to play the forehand drive in this way than the backhand but both can be mastered with the regular practising of correct technique. You must however avoid the excessive use of topspin in driving. Too much spin on the ball reduces its speed and penetration, and much of its advantage is then lost.

90

Once you have topspin drives at your command you also have an effective answer to the volleyer. Passing shots played in this way will dip as they cross the net to provide the opponent with more difficult volleys low down.

Topspin, or rather a combination of sidespin and topspin, is widely used for serving by tournament players. Again the dipping flight of the ball increases the margin for error once the stroke has been well learned, and the ball's awkward swerve through the air and vicious "kick" off the court make the return of service more difficult.

Topspin is best avoided where volleying is concerned but it can be used most effectively on occasions when playing attacking lobs. When time allows, a small amount of topspin on a lob that just clears the opponent's reach will bound away on bouncing and defy return. Although the whipped topspin lob that is now more widely seen in top class tennis can be a spectacular winner as it winds itself up and over the opponent and then down sharply into court, it is a difficult shot to play with consistency.

Use of underspin

A considerable amount of control can be developed when the racket is allowed to

91

slide under the ball to produce underspin. Although as a general rule underspin is less suited for attack than topspin due to the flatter trajectory of the ball, it can provide the extra control that players need in playing such "*touch*" shots as the drop shot, stop volley, and low volley, slow angled passing shots and defensive lobs. This type of spin is also useful in parrying attack by taking the speed off the ball and giving the opponent who likes a "heavy" ball little or nothing to hit.

"*Check*" spin as underspin is sometimes called is obviously needed for shots like the drop-shot and stop-volley. These aim to win the point by holding the ball close to the net and out of the opponent's reach. A less obvious use of underspin is for the approach shot in readiness for volleying against a baseliner who keeps a good length. Such a shot is usually played off the backhand and if not played too hard, its floating flight gives the would-be volleyer more time to move into the close-in volleying position. The defence against a heavy volleying attack is often the underspin lob. Not only does the baseliner develop more accuracy under pressure by "cushioning" and holding the ball on the strings with underspin, but time is also gained for recovery while the ball floats high into the air before bouncing deep into the opponent's court.

92

Volleying, and particularly the low volley, needs underspin to provide the player with the extra control that is needed for these shots. It should not be excessive but just sufficient to allow the player to develop "feel" for accurate placing of the ball.

Use of sidespin and slice

These are of less importance to the player than either topspin or underspin but have their uses for specific shots. The sidespin service for instance is an extremely valuable variation of the flat-hit or topspin varieties. Directed to the left-hand sideline of the service court it can be made to swing away wide out of reach to claim the point there and then or create a positional opening.

Slice is the least used spin probably because it is so limited. A favourite shot though for which it is employed by tournament players is for the forehand approach into the opponent's backhand corner. Not only does it give the net rusher time to get in close but it swings out to the opponent's backhand and stays low on bouncing.

Spin can also be used with telling effect tactically by intelligent players. The grips which some players use for certain shots make them vulnerable either to low balls or to the higher bouncers. Such weaknesses can be exploited through the use of the correct type of spin.

93

Young players are sometimes inclined to play too many of their shots with spin. The highest standards of play are likely to be reached when well controlled basic strokes can occasionally be varied with the astute use of spin. Girls are frequently mystified by its cause and effect. They need not be providing they try first to understand it thoroughly. Not only should all keen players learn how to impart it themselves but they must learn also to judge correctly its effect on the approaching ball. It is not possible to assess spin and its results simply by looking at the ball as it flies towards you. Get to know the actions that are needed to produce the various spins and then learn how to "read" them off your opponent's racket.

94

12 How to play the lob and the drop shot

The lob has always been and still is the most underrated shot in the game. If we could only lob every ball close to the baseline what unbeatable players we should be! Unfortunately although lobbing looks easy it is difficult to produce with consistent accuracy.

A lob of course is a shot played high into the air to fall as close as possible to the opponent's baseline. It can be used offensively when played low over the volleyer who is standing close to the net, and it can be played defensively – as it usually is – when under pressure.

Lobs on both forehand and backhand side are played with similar preparations to the drives. The grips are the same and the main difference is that the racket should drop lower in the backswing so that it can be brought up on the ball at a steeper angle than in driving the ball horizontally. Whenever possible the footwork should also follow the same patterns.

The most common mistakes players make when lobbing are to take their eyes off the ball and to let the wrist go loose through the stroke. Unless you watch the ball closely it is impossible to play it off

the centre of the strings from which a true response can be produced for the fine degree of touch and accuracy this shot requires. Both in forehand and backhand lobbing, keep your backswing compact and your follow-through full and firm-wristed to improve control.

Attacking lobs should be disguised as much as possible as normal drives to gain surprise. Hit them flat or with slight topspin. The exaggerated topspin whip-lob that players like Manuel Santana and Tom Okker have perfected are exceedingly difficult to master.

Defensive lobs are mainly used to parry an opponent's attack. By hitting them fairly high they give you extra time to get into position, and if they are played deep the attack can usually be neutralized.

When the opponent's attacking shot is powerful then greater control can be gained by using underspin on your defensive lobs. Used in this way spin also holds the ball longer in the air, allowing it to drop more vertically into the opposite court thereby helping you to find better length.

Slow-balling an opponent into defeat by the continual use of lobbed returns is perfectly legitimate – if you are good enough to do it. The same tactics can sometimes be used with stunning effect in doubles when more orthodox returns are not proving successful.

The drop-shot

The drop-shot was the last stroke to be developed and exploited in the game. It used to be thought unsporting to use it. Now it is recognized as being of great tactical value. Used correctly but not too often, the softly played and innocuous looking drop-shot is a fearsome weapon in the hands of an expert.

The greatest factor for its success is disguise. Few opponents who are quick on their feet are likely to be caught by even the most accurate shot dropped short over the net if they can see it coming. Try to disguise the drop-shot until the last possible moment by masking it with the normal forehand or backhand drive preparation. Because it must necessarily travel slowly through the air, it should be played off the opponent's shorter returns. And because it must be held as close to the net as possible after bouncing, the drop-shot should be played with underspin. The spin also allows the player to gain greater "feel" and control over the ball as the shot is played.

When you want to play this delicate shot, shape up to the ball in exactly the same manner as you would for the normal drive. Take the racket back but then check it at the top of the backswing, bringing it forwards immediately to slide gently but

97

firmly under the ball with a restricted follow-through. The drop shot therefore is best disguised with a drive preparation but played with a volley type "push" through the ball.

Drop shots that are played too deep into the opponent's court are usually dealt with severely. They can be driven away for winners or counter drop-shot made off them. Experience should teach you the right ball to use for the drop-shot and at the same time you must learn to sense when short returns of your own encourage your opponent to use this stroke. Good length driving is of course the best defence of all against the skilful drop-shotter.

13 Improving your doubles play

For the majority of players doubles is the more entertaining form of tennis. It is physically less demanding than singles but needs more resource and because it is played with a partner it must be played as a team and not just as two individuals on the same side of the net. Men's doubles, when all four players are at the net volleying, is one of the most exciting spectacles the game can provide. Women's doubles are also following the same pattern of serving and volleying these days.

This is the type of play to keep in mind as your aim, but doubles skill can only be developed gradually through experience. When players are able to volley the ball with control they should ensure they stand in the most effective positions on court. The server's partner should be about eight feet from the net and trying to cover as much of the net as possible without leaving the sideline unguarded. The receiver's partner should be on the service line and a few feet inside the court from the sidelines. In this position he is well placed to cover short returns.

Most players usually develop a preference for one particular side of the court. This is an important point to bear in mind when partnerships are being considered. It

is usually best for the player with the superior volley and smash to play in the left court but there are other factors to remember as well. If one player has a much better backhand return of service than the other then he should take the left court. A strong forehand is usually most effective from the right court. Left-handers should normally take the left court and it is better for the man to be on this side in mixed doubles.

Teamwork is an important factor in winning doubles. Understanding your partner's strengths and limitations, just where his returns are most likely to go, and knowing how best to position yourselves during the rallies, comes with experience. Thus better results usually come after partnerships have been in existence for several years.

The server should stand slightly further out from the centre mark than in singles. As a general rule try to keep your service, especially the second ball, on to your opponents' backhands. Few players seem able to do this well but your results will improve enormously when you can start your attack in this way.

The higher the standard of play the more important it is to make sure you win the game each time you serve. Doubles players who are able to serve their first balls into court consistently are usually more successful than those who serve an occasional flashy cannonball followed by several double faults or softly hit second services. When the first service goes in it usually finds the receiver standing further back and consequently less effective returns can be made.

The return of service can also be threatened by an aggressive net player. When your partner is serving and you take up a position at the net, try to put pressure on the receiver if possible by occasionally intercepting his return. One or two of these successfully made may make him take his eye off the ball to see what you are going to do and in any case will keep him in two minds. With this type of pressure acting on the game, the return of service is more difficult in doubles than in singles. Good service returning in doubles means keeping the ball low over the net. If the server follows his service to the net ready to volley your return then try to keep it short to his feet from where he will be forced to volley upwards. Keeping a length to the baseline is less important in doubles except when lobbing.

Volleying comes into doubles play more and more as the standard of play rises. In tournament play doubles is a race between two teams both of whom are trying to establish themselves in a parallel formation close to the net. From this position two

101

good volleyers should be able to command the rallies and the match.

Two courses are open to the opposing team who find themselves being out-generalled in this way. They can try to take up a similar position themselves and dislodge their opponents, or they can stay back and play a more defensive role. This may consist of accurate driving low over the net – and particularly down the middle of the court to test their opponents' teamwork – or they can lob the ball in an effort to drive them back to the baseline.

Mixed doubles

Although mixed doubles is the least important event in high class tournament play it is certainly the most important side of the game as a whole. It offers social advantages few other games can equal. At the highest level mixed doubles are played along similar lines to men's doubles with all four players taking up the attack from the net. In club tennis however the majority of girls cannot expect to match their partners in strength of serving, volleying and smashing. So as a result teamwork and tactics have to be based on a more out-of-balance partnership.

In these circumstances the aim of each side should be to concentrate the play as far as possible on the opposing girl while

102

the men try to shield their partners by covering more than half the court. It leads into tactics and rallies that can be full of fun and excitement.

If the man has the more powerful and effective smash, as is normally the case, the girl must be prepared to step aside when lobs go up that are within her partner's reach. "Poaching" as this is called is sometimes a sore point with partnerships when unsuccessful, but intercepting is normally necessary if the game is not to develop into an uneven match between two players against one. It is of course infuriating for the girl on occasions when her partner dashes across to take the ball off her racket – and misses!

When his partner is serving, the man must sometimes intercept the opposing return of service. Successful interceptions are in the nature of calculated risks because an astute opponent will occasionally direct the ball down the sideline both in the hope of finding that the volleyer has anticipated a cross-court return and also to make him uncertain on future points.

Unlike men's and women's doubles where normally each player should be prepared to cover their own lobs, mixed doubles usually requires the man to chase the deep lobs that are directed over his partner.

Australia's John Newcombe has one of the most powerful and effective services in the game. Note the similarity to the full 'throwing' action. The position of the racket after striking the ball shows that some topspin was used.

Virginia Wade of Great Britain has a powerful forehand drive which in this case is being adapted to a low ball. There is more whip than usual in this stroke resulting in a more restricted follow-through.

The similarity between this stroke and John Newcombe's service should be noted. The backswing for the smash will be seen to be more restricted. Note that when a jump is needed for a ball out of reach, the take-off is from the right foot and the landing made on the left foot.

John Newcombe's forehand drive is typically modern in the way he swings from the shoulder. Note the way he plays his shot off the front foot, keeping his arm and racket in a straight line during the follow-through.

14 Position yourself correctly on court

The two main playing areas in tennis are the backcourt and the forecourt. In the backcourt position you will normally return the ball with your forehand and backhand drives. The forecourt is for the volleying strokes. The backcourt area stretches from the baseline to two or three yards behind it. The forecourt is well inside the service courts – certainly in the forward half of them. Between these two positions lies the dangerous area often known as "no man's land". Generally speaking returns that have to be played from here are more difficult to play effectively. It is important that when you find yourself forced to play a shot from mid-court you should try to return to a safer backcourt or forecourt position again as soon as possible. Many inexperienced players make the mistake of standing still when they have played the ball to see whether it is going into court. Unless you keep on the move and return to a central position near the net or at the baseline you will be badly placed for your next shot.

The receiver's position for returning service should be either just inside or just behind the baseline depending on the speed of the service to be taken. If you are playing in the backcourt it is easier to return the ball when moving forwards than when running backwards. Your shots will also be more effective if you get your body-weight behind them. So stand a few feet behind the baseline and if you have to move forwards inside the court to return the ball, return to your original base after completing the stroke – assuming of course that you wish to continue playing from the backcourt.

A short ball from your opponent of course gives you a wonderful opportunity to attack from the forecourt. If you decide to do this then having played the shorter length ball, move swiftly through "no man's land" to take up the ideal volleying position in the forecourt about eight to ten feet from the net. Players who are learning to follow their service ball to the net for an immediate volleying attack, will find that they are unable to reach this ideal position for the first volley. Try to avoid playing it however from much further back than the service line. Then having successfully played the ball, move forwards again to a safer forecourt position.

During baseline rallies be careful to avoid falling into the trap of playing the ball continually into the open gap when it involves you in playing the ball down the sidelines. Try to play the cross-court

JOHN
NEWCOMBE
SERVICE
STROKE

VIRGINIA
WADE
FOREHAND
DRIVE

JOHN
NEWCOMBE
OVERHEAD
SMASH

JOHN
NEWCOMBE
FOREHAND
DRIVE

shots – where the net is lower – yourself, tempting your opponent to return the ball each time down the lines – where the net is six inches higher. Cross-court driving against an opponent's down-the-line driving also involves him in more running and you in less. Work it out.

The art of positioning yourself correctly gradually develops with experience. It depends not only on a smart appreciation of angles of return but also of your opponents' shots and the effect of wind. As you learn to "read" the play more expertly you will develop another quality which greatly helps your positional sense – anticipation.

106

15 **Practice with a purpose**

It never ceases to astonish me how many players there are who, while giving a great deal of intelligent thought to the competitive side of the game, fail to give any thought at all to methods of practice. They may certainly spend many hours on the practice court but in the majority of cases they either engage in one practice set after another or else hit the ball aimlessly up and down the middle.

Practice is for the purpose of developing the physical and mental techniques and fixing them as habits – turning conscious actions or thoughts into automatic subconscious reactions. If you do something often enough it eventually becomes habitual and thereafter you do it without thinking.

This is the ultimate objective on the practice court. The successful competitor cannot afford to be thinking about how to play the various strokes. All his attention must be given to the match itself – to the placing of the ball, the spin to use, playing to the score, and tactics.

Unfortunately practice does not necessarily make perfect in tennis. Unsound strokes as well as sound ones gradually become automatic if they are practised often enough. The lesson is clear. You must not only practise regularly but you must also be practising the right things. If you are not certain that your game is completely sound, then seek advice from the best coach you can find. But do not forget that a coach is like a doctor. He cannot cure your faults on the spot. What he can do is to diagnose and advise you how to correct any weaknesses you may have. It is up to you to do something about them when you practise.

Regular practice is important but although you should play as much as possible, the *quality* of it is even more important than the quantity. One hour spent with your mind fully engrossed is worth more than ten of purposeless play.

Real determination applied to practice not only brings improvement to your strokes but it gradually deepens your concentration. Such intensity of effort is mentally wearying, and every player has their limitations. Practice should not continue beyond the stage where interest has been lost. Persevere perhaps for another two or three minutes when you feel you would like to stop, to strengthen your concentration and will-power, and then you can relax confident in the knowledge that you have made progress.

So far all the emphasis has been on the mental approach to practice. But what sort of physical routines should be carried out? First, I would suggest that as a general rule you should always concentrate the main part of your practice sessions on weaknesses. If your backhand drive lacks strength and you know the reason why, then start off with a spell on that stroke, putting your mind on to the particular aspect of stroke production you are trying to master. When, after a while, you begin to find your concentration flagging, then refresh your mental approach by switching to something different – your service for instance. Later on before ending your practice stint, return for a second spell on your backhand. In this way your weakness receives a double-helping of attention.

Routine practice exercises

There are a number of routines that I have found to be effective in improving players' strokes and skill. Empty ball box targets placed in various parts of the court are difficult to hit but they emphasize errors of placing and clearly show the degree of control that each player has achieved. Practise each of the four basic drives in turn, first the cross-court forehand and then the cross-court backhand. Then the two shots down the lines can receive attention. Although a direct hit on a box makes a satisfying noise, it is the ability to group the returns that gives the clearest indication of a player's control. The improvement in consistency and accuracy of return after three months of regular practice in this way is often quite remarkable.

For beginners this exercise will be too advanced for the degree of ball control they have achieved. For them initial practice lies in the simple exercise of keeping the rally going. Count all returns that fall inside the lines of the court and then try to increase the number in any one rally. When your control improves make things more difficult by counting only alternate forehand and backhand returns. All sorts of exercises can be contrived by keen players who are determined to improve.

Take the case of the service. Once you have started to master this stroke see how many services out of twenty you can get into the correct court. Later on you can put down ball box targets into the corners and try to serve to them. But do remember that your service swing must be sound. If it is not, then forget all about results and concentrate first on mastering the correct method.

If you have achieved consistency with the simple flat service and wish to develop the spin service then carry out the same step by step procedure. Master the method first without bothering too much about accuracy. Then once you have gained the feeling of the shot go back to progression by results – how many spin serves out of twenty can you get into the service court, and later how close can you direct them to ball box targets. The service is not the easiest stroke but it has one big advantage over all the others. It can be practised on court without the need for an opponent to return it.

When sound stroke-form for the volleys is developing, these strokes can also be developed through specific exercises. Many players feel they are not progressing with their volleys unless they try to hit them with tremendous power. This is over-ambitious thinking. My suggestion is to master basic ball control over the volleys first and then develop their speed later on. So go back to ball box targets in the corners of the baseline and try to group your volley returns as close as possible to each one, much as you have been advised to do with the drives. Successful volleying is in fact mainly the accurate re-direction of your opponent's shot and ball control is essential for this.

In the same way, with two players on the court taking turns to practise and then to "feed" the other, the lob and the smash can receive attention. To obtain maximum benefit, the player practising the smash should return several down the middle of the court for his opponent to return with lobs before the net player goes for a winner to one side or the other.

An astute player can use others well below him in standard for effective practice. He will practise his weaker strokes against his opponent's best shots. Stroke practice does not demand that you must always play against better players.

Value of a practice wall

What nets are to the cricketer and golfer the practice wall can be for tennis player. It unfailingly returns the ball for you to hit. It encourages you to think about your stroke production since no opponent is involved. It is also a highly concentrated form of practice and if carried out properly can produce the equivalent of three sets of play on court in twenty minutes. A white line chalked or painted on the wall at a height of three feet in the centre rising to three feet six inches at each side – to represent the net – can provide the player with the accuracy of result that he most needs to know. Driving, volleying, serving and smashing can all be practised against a wall. Most of the world's best players are fully aware of the way in which this form of practice has helped them to perfect their skill.

16 Correcting common faults

One of the things that helps players to develop their strokes and playing standard is the ability not only to diagnose some of the more common faults they may be making but also to know what to do about correcting them. Coaching is important but not everyone has the opportunity to take lessons with a professional coach. In any case I am also a big believer in self-help once the player has been shown the way. So to assist you to be your own coach I outline some of the faults that I have found to be common to many players.

Lack of power in serving

This is usually the result of an incorrect action. A tendency to "push" at the ball with too firm a wrist is a common cause. Another is a failure to take the racket down behind the head into the "throwing" loop from which racket head speed is developed. To cure these faults try making the wristy throwing action – without the ball – to produce a swishing sound of air through the strings. The louder sound you can make the better. Then try to transfer the same action into the stroke with the ball in play.

Inconsistent results

When one ball goes into the bottom of the net and the next flies too high, the cause is almost certainly erratic placing of the ball in the air. The best way to correct this fault is to develop an awareness of correct positioning of the ball by serving with both feet on the ground throughout the stroke. The finish should see your weight fully forward on the front foot while your right foot "toes" the ground for balance – as at the end of a golf drive. When you find yourself being pulled off balance, check the finish to show you in which way the ball was incorrectly placed. In the forward moving body action of the advanced service, the same *relative* position of ball to the body must be maintained. A few minutes practice of "two footed stance" serving will work wonders with your accuracy in correctly placing the ball.

Erratic direction of the ball

This fault is almost certainly caused by poor control of the racket face during the service stroke. If it is brought to the ball at varying angles then different directions will be imparted to it. Not only must the path of the racket follow a consistent track but so must the angle of the racket face also. An error of only a few degrees either

114

way will result in a considerable error in the ball's direction of flight.

No power in the backhand

This is normally the result of an incorrect shoulder action which makes the player *push* at the ball from the elbow instead of *swinging* at it with power from the back muscles. The root fault is usually poor footwork. The correction is to ensure that your right foot is placed well forwards and across for the stroke. This will encourage a proper turn of the shoulders from which a more powerful swing can be developed.

Power but little control

When the player can produce plenty of power in the backhand stroke but has poor control over the ball, it is usually a case of wrist looseness through the stroke. Check whether you are allowing the head of the racket to drop and slide under the ball at impact. Forget the ball and carry out a few "shadow swings" at normal speed to see what happens to the racket face during your normal swing. Then concentrate on "locking" your wrist through the same "shadow swings". Do you feel a difference? If so then a lack of wrist firmness is your problem to be cured. The same looseness of wrist often brings problems of control in the forehand drive as well.

Lack of control in volleying

When players first attempt to volley and find most of their shots flying way over the baseline, the fault is too long a backswing for the stroke. Until the short take-back of the racket for the volley strokes has been mastered, the player is likely to pull the racket back through habit into the full depth of backswing used in driving. A more compact racket action is required and the player must think in terms of "pushing" through the volleys rather than swinging for them.

Missing or hitting the ball off centre

You are not obeying the most fundamental rule of all – to keep your eye on the ball.

17 Should you change your strokes?

There can hardly be a player who has not at one time or another tried to change a stroke or has contemplated a change. Some who have tried have been successful, others have given up the attempt. All will confirm that changes are usually more difficult than they may seem.

Changing a stroke is not the same as developing a new one. Most players who have sliced backhands and decide to learn the lifted topspin variation are able to develop this new shot. In this case they are learning something new while retaining the old stroke. This involves breaking down one habit and replacing it with another. Typical examples of this are changing grips or in altering the shape of the service swing and racket action.

The problems involved vary from person to person. Young players for instance with their pliable minds, can make changes more easily than seniors. Providing they are patient and determined there is no reason why they should not successfully alter an unsound stroke. For the older player who has probably hit hundreds of thousands of balls in a particular way, changing a stroke presents greater difficulties and even when tackled with great purpose may still occupy a period of several years. For the near beginner of course changes are relatively simple. Habits have not formed deeply and physical movements can be reshaped.

But is it necessary to change a stroke at all? The answer is that no stroke should be changed unless it can be seen to be restricting progress. One example was that of the American Donald Budge whose forehand drive, originally played with a Western grip, handicapped his play on grass courts with their lower bounce. He took a winter off from tournament play, changed to an eastern grip and remodelled his swing, and in due course went on to win the world's first Grand Slam of the four major championships at Wimbledon, and in Paris, New York and Australia.

This is the outstanding example that can be quoted. At the same time I would suggest that every player contemplating a change should satisfy the following rule – if in doubt, don't change.

Three stages are involved in any change. The first is in knowing exactly what you are trying to do and then being able to do it effectively in practice. For talented players this is the simplest stage and rarely takes longer than a day or two. The second stage which is the most difficult is to be able to produce the new stroke *without thinking*. This involves breaking down the old habit and establishing the new one. A learning period of anything from 6 months to 5 years may be necessary. Only then can the player move on to the third stage which is to learn how to use the new stroke to best advantage.

Any player contemplating a change should bear in mind that what may at first seem to be a simple alteration often impinges on other aspects of stroke production. Changing the position of the hand on the handle for instance will immediately affect the angle of the racket face, the shape of the swing that must be made, and almost certainly the footwork as well. Even a different stance for serving will trigger off a chain reaction of adaptations that will have to be made.

If the impression I have given to any player contemplating a change is one of extreme caution it is only to present clearly the difficulties that exist. Anyone who has tried to change and has given up the task may well find his original stroke has lost its previous effect. My suggestion is that a qualified professional coach should always be consulted before a start is made.

18 How to plan and play a match

Planning a match should start well before you step on to court. A careful preparation is necessary to ensure your own readiness and fitness and to provide you with an initial plan of action.

It is surprising how many players, particularly juniors, give their approaching matches hardly more than a passing thought other than to toss a few clothes and a racket into a tennis case and set off hopefully to play it.

The first thing is to make sure that all your equipment is in good order and suitable for the contest ahead. Many a match has been lost because a frayed string has snapped during play and broken the player's confidence and concentration. It is important to know what type of court surface your match is likely to be played on. This will give you an opportunity to practise on it beforehand and to make sure your tennis shoes are suitable. Smooth soled ones for example are fine on dry grass, concrete and tarmacadam surfaces, but they will not give you a secure foothold on loose surface hard courts that are now widely used. On this type of court a ridged sole or one with a serrated pattern gives a much better grip in getting off the mark and changing direction quickly.

Always wear clothes that give you free-dom of movement and feel comfortable to the point where you can forget all about them. Tight shorts or frilly dresses that billow in a breeze are likely to affect your concentration. Don't forget to carry a hand towel with you to wipe away perspiration and keep your playing hand dry. Some players use resin or sawdust for this pur-pose and carry a supply around with them.

If you are going to play in a tournament then balls will almost certainly be provided. But if your match is an individual one then either you or your opponent will have to supply some. The normal procedure is for the "home" player to provide them for the guest. Four are sufficient but make sure they are in good condition and not soft or worn smooth.

Now you are all ready to play but have you given thought to the tactics you should adopt against your opponent? Obviously to do this you must have some knowledge of your opponent's game. The more detailed this is the easier it is to plan successfully. What should you look for?

First consider your opponent's stroke play. Has he a strong service? What sort of second service can he produce – flat or spin? Is his backhand weak in a rally or only when put under pressure from an attack from the net? Has he good passing shots or a good lob – or both? Does he like to volley and if so is his backhand volley as sound as his forehand? Can he smash? Is he quick about the court or can you score with drop-shots? Does he play better against a hard hitter or a slow baller? These are only some of the stock questions about your opponents that need to be answered before you can expect to come up with the right answer tactically.

Then do not forget that an opponent's strengths and weaknesses do not end with an assessment of strokes and technique. Some players perform well only when they are winning. Get them in a tough fight and they crack. Others play better when they are behind and against this type of opponent you must be careful not to become over confident or relax when you are winning. Conversely some players become careless when they are in the lead, so never give up however hopeless your task may appear.

The use of sound tactics also depends on a completely accurate assessment of your own strengths and weaknesses. If, for example, you know your opponent's backhand is likely to crack under the pressure of a volleying attack, it is foolish to plan such tactics if your own skill in volleying is lacking. The best tacticians are those who can most skilfully apply their best shots against their opponent's weaknesses while shielding their own.

Suppose however, that you find yourself in the position of having to play an opponent you have never seen in action before. How do you start to plan your tactics then?

On such occasions the pre-match practice is a vital time to glean as much information as possible. If your opponent's forehand and backhand drives appear to be well balanced, a good way of discovering which is the weaker is to hit the ball straight to your opponent. It will be second nature for him to step around and play it on the side he prefers.

While tuning up your own strokes give your opponent an assortment of returns both wide and down the middle of the court. Players usually have a preference and few play both types with equal ease. Change the speed of your returns as well to see the reaction.

Most of the information about your opponent's game will be learnt as the game progresses. Keep cool and calm and collect all the knowledge you can, planning your tactics by trial and error. But once you have hit on a plan which is proving successful, avoid the temptation to experiment as by doing so you may possibly allow your opponent the chance to wriggle off the hook.

The golden rule of successful match play is never to change winning tactics, but always to change losing ones.

Forehand volley
Virginia Wade

Note the alert preparation. The eyes are on the approaching ball and the left hand is being used for balance as the shoulders turn to take the racket back. At this stage the bodyweight should be on the back (right) foot.

Watching and judging the flight of the ball. The head of the racket is held well up as it starts to come forward. The bodyweight is well forwards and the extended left arm continues to aid balance.

The ball has been struck but the eyes continue to follow it closely. The firm wrist keeps the head of the racket well up. Note that as the left foot comes forwards to receive the bodyweight, the shoulders are also turning as the follow-through begins.

The wrist is kept quite firm to control the racket face into the finish. The bodyweight has come forwards fully but good balance has been maintained. From this stage the recovery will be made quickly to the 'ready' position.

Forehand volley
Roger Taylor

The ball in Taylor's right hand suggests that he is following a service to the net. Note his crouching approach as he sees the ball coming towards his forehand side. As with all good volleyers, Taylor keeps the head of the racket well up and his wrist firm.

Shaping up for the volley. Note the restricted take-back of the racket, the balancing right arm and the way the bodyweight is moving forwards on to the front (right) foot. This is the time when the ball must be watched closely.

The weight is perfectly balanced. Note the correct 'pushing' action, and also the firmly controlled racket face. Taylor has got down to this low ball by bending at his knees so that he can keep the head of the racket well up at impact.

Taylor's great strength which aids his control can be seen in the finish to this stroke. His weight is now on the front foot and he is perfectly balanced to make a quick recovery to the "ready" position for the next shot he may have to play.

High forehand volley
Virginia Wade

The ideal "ready" position with the racket centrally positioned and its head held well up. The knees are slightly bent to assist speed off the mark. The feet are spread to assist sideways court coverage.

The ball is high up so the take-back of the racket is high. The eyes are on the ball, the left hand is aiding balance and the body-weight ready to move forwards off the back (right) foot.

The racket is being brought slightly downwards to the ball as it is struck giving the impression that the ball was struck off centre. Note how the player's eyes are still on the ball and the way the wrist is being kept firm right through the shot. . .

. . . and into the finish. The shoulders have turned into the stroke as the bodyweight goes forwards on to the left foot. From this perfectly balanced position a quick recovery to the original "ready" position can be made.

Backhand volley
Virginia Wade

Virginia Wade is moving into the first stage of the stroke from the facing the net "ready" position. Note the early turn of the shoulders which takes the racket back. Her weight is on the back (left) foot ready to be tumbled forwards. . .

. . . as the stroke is played. The ball is obviously going to be a low one and the racket face is already open for the underspin the low volley needs for control. Care in watching the ball at this stage is vital.

By bending well at the knees and keeping her back straight, Virginia shows how the racket head can be kept well up for greater control and balance is more easily maintained. The left arm also helps balance and should be fully extended.

"Stay down" with the ball on a low volley until the stroke has been completed. Provided that good balance has been held during the shot, a quick recovery can be made to the original facing the net "ready" position.